How have things changed?

Holidays

James Nixon

W

FRANKLIN WATTS
LONDON · SYDNEY

This edition published in 2012 by
Franklin Watts
338 Euston Road
London NW1 3BH

Franklin Watts Australia
Level 17/207 Kent Street
Sydney NSW 2000

ISBN: 978 1 4451 0792 9

Dewey classification number: 790.1

A CIP catalogue record for this book is available
from the British Library.

Planning and production by Discovery Books Limited
Editor: James Nixon
Designer: Rob Norridge

Photographs: p6 (top) Mary Evans Picture Library, p6 (bottom) T.E. Cobb/Mary Evans Picture Library, p7
(top) Chris Fairclough, p7 (bottom) Chris Fairclough/ CFWimages.com, p9 (top) Chris Fairclough, p10
Mary Evans Picture Library, p11 Chris Fairclough, p12 (top) Mary Evans Picture Library, p12 (bottom)
Duncan Walker/istockphoto.com, p13 (top) Corbis, p13 (bottom) Steve Rabin/istockphoto.com, p14 The
Royal Pavilion and Museums, Brighton and Hove, p15 Chris Fairclough, p16 Mary Evans Picture
Library, p17 Bobby Humphrey, p18 (top) E. Bacon/Getty Images, p18 (bottom) Science and Society
Picture Library, p19 (top) Mary Evans Picture Library, p19 (bottom) Maurice van der Velden/
istockphoto.com, p20 (top) Felix Man/Getty Images, p20 (right) The Advertising Archives, p20 (bottom)
Bert Hardy/Getty Images, p21 Center Parcs, p22 Courtesy of Derbyshire County Council and
www.picturethepast.org.uk, p23 (top) Roger G Howard Photography, p23 (bottom) Fforest Fields
Campsite, p24 S.B. Davie/Mary Evans Picture Library, p25 (top) Vera Bogaerts/istockphoto.com, p25
(bottom) Tammy Peluso/istockphoto.com, p26 Getty Images, p27 (top) David Pedre/istockphoto.com,
p27 (bottom) Jirko Kazakov/istockphoto.com.

Cover photos: (top) Mary Evans Picture Library, (bottom) Corbis.

Printed in China

Franklin Watts is a division of Hachette Children's Books,
an Hachette UK company
www.hachette.co.uk

Contents

How have holidays changed?

When did you go on your last holiday? Did you go abroad, or holiday in this country? Where did your parents go on holiday when they were children?

1905

1930

Charles D. Smith
· PUNCH & JUDY ·
PERFORMANCES · 11ᴬᴹ 3ᴾᴹ & 7ᴾᴹ

This book will look at how holidays have changed in the last 100 years. These pictures show people on holiday at the seaside in the early part of the twentieth century.

Then and now

Look at the pictures on both pages. What differences between then and now can you see? What similarities are there?

Now look at the pictures below showing seaside scenes today. Holidays have changed in many ways, but lots of things have stayed the same.

Now

At some seaside **resorts**, you still find donkey rides on offer, and a Punch and Judy show, just as your great grandparents did in the past.

Now

Where to go

In the past, most people spent their holidays in Britain. Seaside holidays were very popular.

View of Brighton Beach.

This postcard shows Brighton in **Victorian** times. Many families then could not afford a week's holiday. They would usually visit the seaside for one or two days.

By the 1950s people were taking longer holidays. This postcard from 1955 shows holidaymakers on Eastbourne beach in the south of England.

1955

THREE PROMENADES, GRAND PARADE, EASTBOURNE.

Nowadays a lot of people go abroad for their holiday. Aeroplanes can take you to anywhere in the world.

Many people choose to go to other countries because the weather is sunnier and warmer. This modern postcard has been sent from the island of Crete in Greece.

CRETE - HERSONISSOS

Now

Find out for yourself

Ask your friends where they went on their last summer holiday. Draw a bar graph to show where everyone went.

9

On the beach

A hundred years ago people would not have dreamt of taking their clothes off on the beach.

Look at this photo taken in 1910. Men wore smart suits and the women wore long dresses and hats.

1910

LOWESTOFT FROM THE SOUTH

If you wanted to paddle you would take off your shoes and socks, and roll up your trousers or dress.

Today, holidaymakers wear fewer clothes on the beach.
In this photo many people are wearing bathing costumes.

Now

People now wear **sunscreen**, hats and sunglasses to protect themselves from the sun. How else are the people on the beach above keeping out of the sun?

Then and now

These children have taken their buckets and spades on to the sand to build sandcastles. Look back at the photo on the opposite page. Did people use buckets and spades in 1910?

Swimming

If you wanted to swim in the sea a hundred years ago you got changed inside a wooden hut called a bathing machine. This way people were not seen wearing only a swimming costume.

Look at this photo from 1905. Bathing huts were on wheels so they could be pulled down to the sea.

1905

4226 B.

1900

Look how large and baggy the swimming costumes were in the 1900s.

People still like to swim and splash around in the sea. The sea is now used for other sports as well. Sailing, surfing and **windsurfing** are very popular.

Now

Now

In this picture children are playing with inflatable toys and **dinghies**. Most beaches now have a lifeguard who makes sure that people are safe in the water.

Then and now

Compare these swimming costumes (above) to the ones in 1900. Which costumes do you think would be more comfortable to swim in?

Piers and promenades

Many people who went to the seaside a hundred years ago did not go onto the beach. They were happy just to stroll along the **promenades** and **pier**.

1910

Piers and promenades offered all sorts of entertainment. Look at Brighton pier in 1920. What entertainment can you see being **advertised**?

1920

Now

This is Brighton pier today. Many seaside resorts still have a pier offering shows and entertainments.

Then and now

Look at the photo above and compare it to the old pictures on the last page. How has the pier changed?

Now look at the promenade in Brighton today. It still gets very busy in the summer. What attractions can you see on the promenade?

Funfairs and amusements

Fairgrounds with children's rides and games have been popular at the seaside since Victorian times.

Then and now

Can you find these rides at fairgrounds today?

1915

Most resorts had a helter skelter, which was a long and twisting slide. This is a photo of the Pleasure Beach funfair in Blackpool in 1915.

In the past **slot-machine** games at the seaside were mechanical. You pulled levers or turned handles to make them work.

1960s

This woman is playing a machine called a one-armed bandit. Why do you think it was called this?

Fairground rides have got more exciting over the years. Look at the photo of Blackpool Pleasure Beach today. It has lots of fast-moving rollercoasters. Some take you high into the sky. Others toss you from side to side or turn you upside down.

How do you think the people on this rollercoaster feel?

Now

Now

Slot machines in **amusement arcades** today are electronic, and are played by pressing buttons. Some games give you the chance of winning cuddly toys.

Getting there

By the twentieth century there were railways across Britain. Trains made it quick and easy for people to get to the coast.

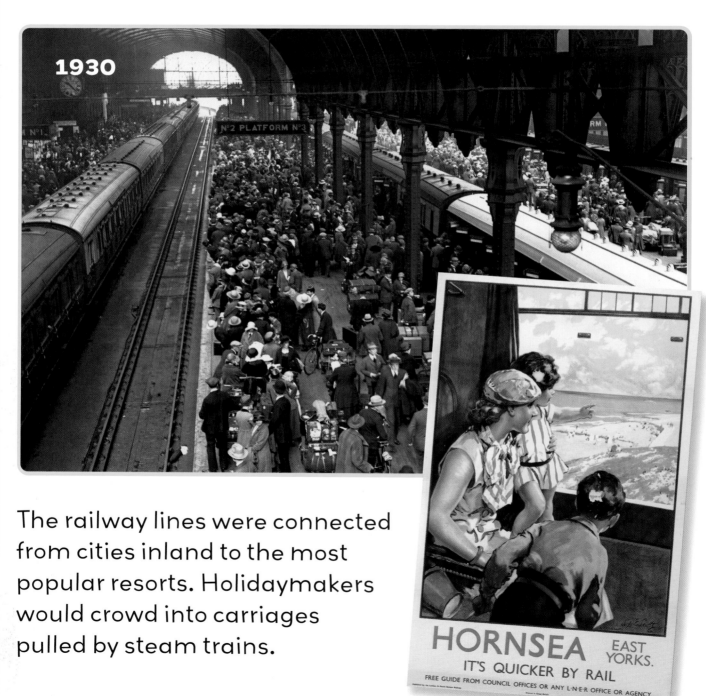

1930

N° 2 PLATFORM N° 3

HORNSEA EAST YORKS.
IT'S QUICKER BY RAIL
FREE GUIDE FROM COUNCIL OFFICES OR ANY L·N·E·R OFFICE OR AGENCY

The railway lines were connected from cities inland to the most popular resorts. Holidaymakers would crowd into carriages pulled by steam trains.

1918

In the past, it was common for people to go to the seaside in big groups. Families would take aunts, uncles and grandparents. Sometimes everyone from the same street or factory would go away together.

In the early twentieth century, families and large groups travelled to the seaside in **charabancs** like these.

Since the 1960s, most people have had their own transport. Today, the roads are full of traffic. Trying to get to the coast in the summer can be slow and tiring. We don't tend to go on holiday in large groups any more.

Then and now

Do you think holiday travel was more fun in the past?

Now

Holiday camps

1939

By the 1950s most people could afford a longer holiday. Holiday camps were set up by Billy Butlin and others to entertain people for a whole week.

The camps provided food, entertainment and **chalets** to sleep in. They also had a swimming pool and a funfair. Games such as the knobbly knees and glamorous granny competitions were organised by the staff.

The children in this picture are playing 'follow the pirate'.

1953

The British holiday camp is not as popular as it used to be. Many families want to spend time alone on holiday and entertain themselves.

Some people still holiday at camps. Center Parcs have opened up holiday villages in the countryside, which are similar to camps. They have **facilities** like restaurants, boating lakes, swimming pools and cycle hire.

Then and now

Where would you rather spend your holiday – Butlin's or Center Parcs? Why?

Going to the countryside

Holidays in the countryside were less common in the past than they are today because fewer people had transport.

Then and now

Compare the tents in the old and new photographs. Which would you rather spend the night in?

1936

However, some people did go camping. Look at the holidaymakers in this photo taken in 1936. Even on a camping holiday people wore their smartest clothes. Do you think wearing these clothes on a camping holiday was comfortable?

Today, travelling around is so much easier that people can visit anywhere they like on holiday. Countryside holidays are now very common. Lots of people tour the countryside in a motor caravan.

Look at the picture of the family on a campsite today. They are using modern equipment such as a gas cooker and a fold-up picnic bench. It can all be easily transported in the car.

Now

Flying away

Holiday air travel began in the 1930s but only the very rich could travel by plane. By the 1970s flying had become a lot cheaper. More people took their holidays abroad.

Package holidays to sunny countries like Spain and Greece became very popular. The package offered the air travel, food and hotel all in one.

1968

This picture shows British tourists in 1968. They are sunbathing on the beach at Benidorm in Spain.

More and more people are now taking their holidays abroad. Greece and Spain are still popular places to visit. But many people now wish to explore more unusual and **exotic** places.

Then and now

The British now make over 40 million holiday trips abroad in a year. In 1970, that figure was just over 4 million.

Now

These holidaymakers are on a **tropical** beach in Thailand.

This family is snorkelling in the sea off a Caribbean island.

How many places mentioned on this page can you find on a map or globe?

Winter holidays

Many people fifty years ago could not afford a summer holiday, never mind a winter holiday.

1955

If people did take an extra holiday it would often be a day trip to a British city. Only very wealthy people went skiing abroad. Look at this family (above) on a winter holiday in 1955.

Then and now

Look on the next page at the clothes people wear skiing today. How do they compare to the clothes in this picture?

Today, many more people can afford to take a holiday in the winter as well as the summer. Some people go abroad to warmer countries to escape the British winter.

Why is there nobody sitting in the chairlifts on the left-hand side of this picture?

Now

Others go to snowy countries for a skiing holiday. This boy is having skiing lessons with other children who are on holiday.

Glossary

Advertised Described on a poster or billboard to attract customers.

Amusement arcades Indoor areas that contain slot-machine games.

Chalets Wooden houses in a holiday camp.

Charabanc An early form of bus used for holiday trips.

Dinghies Small inflatable boats.

Exotic Describes places that are unusual and a long distance away.

Facilities Equipment or services provided for people.

Pier A large platform which sticks out into the sea and which people can walk along.

Promenades Roads or paths next to the sea at a seaside resort.

Resorts Places that are commonly visited for a holiday.

Slot machine A machine worked by putting a coin in it.

Sunscreen A cream rubbed on to the skin to protect it from the sun.

Tropical Having hot and humid weather for most of the year.

Windsurfing The sport of moving along the surface of the sea by standing on a board with a sail on it.

Victorian Relating to the reign of Queen Victoria, which lasted from 1837 to 1901.

Further information

Places to visit:

The seaside!
Many UK seaside towns became popular holiday destinations in the 19th century and have lots of history to explore – mentioned in this book are Blackpool, Brighton, Eastbourne, Lowestoft and Hornsea (East Yorkshire).

The V&A Museum of Childhood, London (www.vam.ac.uk/moc)
This museum is all about the history of childhood and includes a section on holidays in the past.

Websites:

www.snaithprimary.eril.net/rather.htm
has a slideshow of seaside holiday photos through the ages

www.crickweb.co.uk/assets/resources/flash.php?&file=seaside
is a seaside history site that has interactive activities for you to do

www.nationalarchives.gov.uk/education/victorianbritain/happy/default.htm
explores how the railways changed Britain, with particular reference to holidays and leisure activities

www.tlfe.org.uk/prometheanflipchartsforhistory
is a section on the Lighthouse for Learning website which offers flip charts on a variety of history topics, including the Victorian seaside

Books to read:

Holidays by the Sea: Past and Present, Catherine Allison, 2002 (Longman)

Holidays Then and Now, Brian Moses, 2002 (Collins)

The Seaside (History Snapshots), Sarah Ridley, 2007 (Franklin Watts)

Seaside Holidays (Start-Up History), Stewart Ross, 2002 (Evans)

Seaside Holidays (Ways into History), Sally Hewitt, 2004 (Franklin Watts)

Victorian Seaside Holidays (Life in the Past), Mandy Ross, 2005 (Heinemann)

Index